10 INDISPENSABLE **PRACTICES** OF

THE **2**-MINUTE
LEADER

BRIAN
DODD

Spire Resources, Inc.
PO Box 180
Camarillo, CA 93011
1-800-992-3060
www.spire-resources.com

ISBN 978-1-935843-37-5

Printed in the United States of America

CONTENTS

INTRODUCTION

I never expected to be an author. Beyond that, I never expected to be a blogger with thousands of faithful readers. Yet here I am, writing to you as both a first-time author and a long-time blogger. When I began working on this book my strategy was simple and straightforward: Assemble the best of my blog posts and edit them into a cohesive collection. But that's not what happened. The project started out that way but then something very unexpected occurred: In re-reading and re-thinking virtually everything I had posted on my site over a period of several years, I discovered a treasure that I didn't even know was there. Woven into the fabric of those writings were unifying concepts, like parallel golden threads running from one edge to the other. I saw that they were not principles but practices—core habits of the successful leader. And I realized that I had been implementing those practices day-in and day-out in my own leadership roles for a long time. With increasing brightness they came to light in perfect clarity—and once I saw them, I knew that those practices would be the subject of this book.

Although I didn't begin with a specific target in mind, I was pleased when the list of key practices ended up being a perfect 10. And right from the outset I could see how those 10 formed a natural progression. It occurred to me that the original title I had chosen for the book would have to be modified to fit the new structure and content; but that turned out to be a relatively minor adjustment. The working title had been *The 2-Minute Leader: Daily Power Bursts of Insight & Inspiration*. The first part of that title—*The 2-Minute Leader*—derived from a simple characteristic: It takes about two minutes to read a typical post on my blog, and nearly every post has something to do with leadership. Thus, *The 2-Minute Leader*. As I thought about changing the title another revelation dawned: All 10 practices can be rapidly activated and applied. And most of the time, two minutes is ample time to at least start the process of implementation. The new title all but dictated itself:

10 Indispensable Practices of
The 2-Minute Leader

I went to work—polishing and perfecting the list of practices and then matching them up with a selection of blog posts corresponding to each theme. That turned out to be quite a challenge because the content from my blog posts had to be edited to fit the flow of the book. The 10 chapters ultimately incorporated parts of more than 50 blog posts. The posts proved to be a rich source of illustrations, ideas and insights; and as the material was combined and put into a new form and format it gained new strength and substance. If you've been a regular reader of my blog—*Brian Dodd on Leadership*—you will undoubtedly read with a sense of déjà vu. At the same time, you will sense that what may seem familiar is actually quite different.

Each of the 10 Indispensable Practices centers on a key word, a key statement and a key application. You will experience each one in depth over the course of the book, but here's a quick run-down:

Practice #1: DREAMING. Double-Dare Yourself. When faced with an opportunity that will stretch your capacity or a challenge that will call for an extraordinary effort, say to yourself: *"I dare myself to...."* Complete the statement; then set about fulfilling that opportunity or meeting that challenge.

Practice #2: THINKING. Take Two Every Day, as Often as Needed. Spend two minutes focused in thinking about the biggest thing you're facing.

Practice #3: RELATING. Keep a Leadership Ledger. Create it wisely. Review it daily. Update it frequently.

Practice #4: ENLISTING. Look to a Person's Past, Present and Potential. When hiring, assigning or reviewing, let a person's past inform you, their present instruct you, and their potential inspire you.

Practice #5: POSITIONING. Align the Elements. Strategically position every key project with key preparations and key people.

Practice #6: COMMUNICATING. Communicate Expectations, Directions and Commendations. Communicate expectations before the fact. Communicate directions within the bounds. Communicate commendation without hesitation.

Practice #7: EXECUTING. Take AIM. Activate your plan. **I**ntegrate your resources. **M**obilize your team.

Practice #8: ADJUSTING. Check Your Bearings and Adjust as Needed. Stay alert to changing conditions and ready to make course corrections.

Practice #9: PERSEVERING. Name It and Declaim It. Identify whatever threatens to pull you down and deny its power over you.

Practice #10: CELEBRATING. ACT Positively. Acknowledge excellence. **C**elebrate achievement. **T**ransform relationships.

I had anticipated creating an entirely different kind of book. At the outset, I thought I had it all figured out; and I had already spent scores of hours working on that original plan before something totally different emerged. It was tough to say good-bye to all that labor and say hello to a new approach that would doubtless be even more demanding. But I did, and I was soon living out as never before the very practices described above. I definitely had to adjust and I had to persevere; and because I did, I am celebrating as I write these words today.

My hope is that your life and your leadership will be enriched and energized by these *10 Indispensable Practices of The 2-Minute Leader.* I encourage you to not simply read these pages but to adopt these practices. Take some time to honestly assess where you are as a leader and determine how you can best intensify your strengths and minimize your weaknesses. Make a commitment to yourself to never accept the status quo. You have more potential and promise than you even imagine. Harness that potential and claim that promise as you pursue excellence in every role and responsibility. As you do so, I am absolutely confident that these practices can make an amazing difference and an indelible impact.

May God bless your journey!

Brian Dodd

Practice #1
DREAMING
Double-Dare Yourself.

When faced with an opportunity that will stretch
your capacity or a challenge that will call for extraordinary effort, say to yourself: "I dare myself to...."
Complete the statement; then set about
fulfilling that opportunity or meeting that challenge.

Are you a dreamer? A risk taker? Do you go for
broke? Do you swing for the fences? Are you a bold
visionary?

I know a number of people who can without a
millisecond's hesitation answer *Yes* to all of those
questions. They don't just think constantly—they
think big, very big. Perhaps you're one of that special
breed. Not me. In fact, I'm as vanilla as they come.
If you think I'm being inordinately humble, think
again. Here are some facts to prove my point:

- I've had the same haircut since 1980.

- I only wear blue, black, red and white.

- Both of my cars are paid off.

- Rarely do I go into debt.

- Even in my 40s, I still say "Yes, Sir" and "No, Sir."

- I never drive more than seven miles an hour over the speed limit.

- I wave others through at a four-way stop.

- I stared at the iPad for six months and still had not pulled the trigger to buy one.

- I have lived within a 20-mile radius my entire life.

A good friend told me, "Brian, you are one stable human being." That was meant as a compliment; and I appreciate the kind words. At the same time, I recognize that only a single consonant separates *stable* from *stale*. Stable is good. Stale is bad. And the way to avoid staleness is through strategic intentionality. Here's what I mean by that: There are some very desirable qualities like reliability, faithfulness and consistency that come with stability. But as a leader and a person, to stay fresh I have to strategically and intentionally push myself to go above and beyond the expected and the obvious.

> *To stay fresh I have to strategically and intentionally push myself to go above and beyond the expected and the obvious.*

Like the typical boy growing up in America, I had my share of friends who were constantly daring one another to do all manner of bold or outlandish things. One friend in particular would say, "I dare you!" If the dare was resisted, he would then say, "I double-dare you!" Like many kids, I began to associate daring with recklessness. It wasn't until much later in life that I learned the positive side of a daring spirit.

I'm privileged to know a lot of visionary leaders, and to a person they are all daring—willing to take risks, to push the envelope, to test the limits of personal capacity. They dare themselves to go above and beyond, and they inspire me to do likewise. Many of them, of course, will admit that they are inherently very much like I am—naturally reticent to extend the boundaries of normal. And, like me, they have learned that it's possible to train the mind and heart to be daring. It was certainly necessary for me to cultivate the two-minute practice of daring myself—precisely because it is not my natural inclination.

> *It was necessary for me to cultivate the two-minute practice of daring myself—precisely because it is not my natural inclination.*

As I've put this practice into motion I've recently had some serious brain-to-heart talks with myself and some intense conversations with God. I have dared myself to do several things:

• To invest hard-earned capital in what I believe to be a great idea—without the guarantee of a return.

• To welcome tough conversations, not back away from them.

14

• To be more vulnerable and transparent in key relationships.

• To be more intentional about cultivating friendships.

• To share my faith more readily with more people who have yet to experience the love of Jesus.

• To take my wife to places around the world she never expected to go.

• To go skydiving...maybe.

• To swim with the great whites (in a shark cage, of course).

• To get a trendy haircut. Though, now that I think about it, maybe that would be going too far!

For someone like me, these are big statements to make; but I know that each one will pay dividends in my life and my leadership. The more my vision broadens, the more I can cast vision to those whom I lead. I want to dream bigger dreams and dare to do greater things for God's glory. I was inspired recently in reading about Francis Xavier, a Christian missionary of the 16th century who took the Good News of Jesus to

India, Japan, Borneo, the Moluccas and other lands. He sent a co-worker back to Europe with this challenge: "Tell the students to give up their small ambitions and come eastward to preach the Gospel of Christ." I love that one phrase in his statement: "...give up their small ambitions...." It motivates me to give up any small dreams that I harbor and to reach for something greater, something truly significant.

These are hard things to contemplate in a culture permeated with the desire for comfort. I read recently about the burgeoning popularity of "glamping"—short for "glamorous camping." Instead of truly camping, "glampers" choose to live in luxury when they're out in the wilds of nature. It's catching on. KOA Kampgrounds reports a 26% increase in luxury lodge rentals. Ruben Martinez of Glamping Hub says, "After a week you're not thinking, 'I look homeless right now.' You're thinking about how comfortable you are."[1]

Whether at my desk, around a conference table, in my community, at my church or in the great outdoors, I don't want to be obsessed with how comfortable I am. In fact, I want to get out of my comfort zone because that's when I grow as a person and as a leader. Far too many leaders (and aspiring leaders) have become far too comfortable. In numerous conversations and in countless observations, I have seen the signs...

1. They are not living and leading with a high level of expectancy.

2. They have a diminished concern for the spiritual condition of neighbors, family members or co-workers.

3. They haven't had a spiritual conversation with a non-Christian in a long time.

> *I don't want to be obsessed with how comfortable I am. In fact, I want to get out of my comfort zone because that's when I grow as a person and as a leader.*

4. They read the Bible but it seems like a history book to them.

5. Their comfort on a Sunday morning is more important than what it takes to reach the unchurched. As long as they get to their parking spot, their seat, and hear the music they like, everything's just fine.

6. They aren't fazed by people in desperate need.

7. Reports or even stark photos of suffering children do not move them to action.

8. They don't give financial resources readily or sacrificially.

9. Their prayers don't seem to be making it past the ceiling.

10. It doesn't even dawn on them that God could do something revolutionary in their life this very day.

Many of these descriptions have fit my life at various times. Like the "glampers" who want to rough it without roughing it, I have often become lulled into far too comfortable a mindset. Can you relate?

When Jesus chose his core disciples, he called them to leave everything and risk everything in order to gain everything in relationship to him. After his resurrection and their spiritual empowerment on the Day of Pentecost, their training was done. Eleven faithful ones remained; and never again did they play it safe. At this point in my life I really want to be like them. I want to follow Jesus, to take risks, to think differently, to not settle for what is safe. What about you?

A high percentage of the leaders to whom I relate day in and day out are pastors. I talk with them, pray with them, counsel them; and I often encourage them to listen to that still, small inner voice that dares them to go beyond what is typical—to dare to live and lead in a bold way. Many of them have done so, and their churches have felt the impact.

> *When Jesus chose his core disciples he called them to leave everything and risk everything in order to gain everything in relationship to him.*

Some have dared to challenge their congregations to become multi-cultural, multi-generational, even multi-lingual.

Some have dared to call their people to make huge financial commitments to causes that will go on beyond the lifetime of the givers.

Some have dared their people to embrace social media not for purposes of self-gratification and entertainment but for the sake of real ministry.

Some have dared their churches to become places of community service and outreach 24 hours a day.

Some have dared their fellow Christians to reach out to the outcasts of society, to open their hearts and extend their hands to the hurting, the poor, the lonely, the devalued, the under-privileged.

Some have dared to dream of their church being so radically Christian in word, deed and attitude that people take notice—not of the believers themselves, but of the Lord they serve.

Whatever your temperament, whether you're a born dreamer and risk taker or one on the opposite end of the spectrum, this two-minute practice is for you. All of us—regardless of our natural inclination—will be faced with opportunities that will stretch our capacity or challenges that will call for extraordinary effort. In meeting each one, learn to say to yourself: *"I dare myself to...."* Then complete the statement and set about fulfilling the opportunity or meeting the challenge. Your life will be enriched and your leadership will be extended in new and unexpected ways.

> *All of us—regardless of our natural inclination—will be faced with opportunities that will stretch our capacity or challenges that will call for extraordinary effort.*

Practice #2
THINKING
Take Two Every Day, as Often as Needed.
Two minutes—totally focused in thinking
about the biggest thing you're facing.

"Thinking is the hardest work there is, which is probably the reason so few engage in it." So said Henry Ford, one of the fathers of the American automobile industry.

A legendary leader from our own generation, Apple founder Steve Jobs, said, "Simple can be harder than complex: You have to work hard to get your thinking clean to make it simple. But it's worth it in the end because once you get there, you can move mountains."[1]

To my knowledge, Steve Jobs never professed to be a Christ follower. But his words echo a phrase from the teachings of Jesus: "I tell you the truth, if you had faith even as small as a mustard seed, you could say to this mountain, 'Move from here to there,' and it would move. Nothing would be impossible."[2] To me, the parallel in these statements—one by Jobs, and the other by Jesus—is significant because concentrated, uncomplicated thinking has a direct link to concentrated, uncomplicated faith. If you believe clearly, you can think clearly. If you have a strong faith, you can experience strong thoughts.

I have observed that great leaders are almost always great thinkers. I study their lives and find myself wondering... *What are they focusing their attention on? What questions are they asking? What books are they reading? Who are they talking to? What are they doing? What are they not doing?* And the one I wonder about most often: *What new ideas are they coming up with and what will come from those ideas?*

> "*Great leaders are almost always great thinkers.*"

The power and value of concentrated thought cannot be overestimated. It is a hallmark of disciplined, decisive leaders. This indispensable practice taps into that power. Believe me, two minutes of uninterrupted, totally focused thinking about the biggest thing you're facing can pay off in a big way. It's like a pit-stop for an Indy car in the middle of a roaring race: it only takes a very short time, but so much more can be accomplished and so much power can be gained to run the race with even greater energy and precision.

When it comes to harnessing the power of your thoughts, keep these things in mind:

1. Great thoughts are enhanced by concentration, but they can come from anywhere at any time. Pay attention and be ready to capture them.

2. Great thoughts sometimes get better when re-processed and re-positioned by others. Don't hold onto your thoughts as if they were your exclusive property. Use them to add value to others' lives.

3. Great thoughts have staying power. Don't give up on what you are convinced is a breakthrough idea.

4. Great thoughts generate other thoughts. In fact, the secondary concept may be the greater one.

5. Great thoughts that come with concentration can often be enhanced through collabora-

tion. Tap into the thinking of smart people around you and let them tap into yours.

6. Great thoughts hold the promise of benefit to others. Be internally disciplined in your thinking but externally focused in your doing.

7. Great thoughts can come in a burst but they are usually not fully formed upon arrival. Take time to process and refine them.

8. Great thoughts often need even more thinking before they become reality. Be ready to plan and act on them accordingly.

9. Great thoughts are always needed. Devote time every day to uninterrupted, unimpeded thinking.

10. Great thoughts are valuable. Once they are properly developed, ideas have worth and sustainability.

For a leader, working hard is critical; but thinking hard is crucial. To think as effectively as possible, I urge you to form the habit of the two-minute hyper-focus on the biggest thing facing you at any chosen moment. As you do so, keep in mind that simplicity is paramount.

> *For a leader, working hard is critical; but thinking hard is crucial.*

I recently heard a prominent leader say, "I have complexity. I need simplicity." Indeed, life can get very complicated. We are constantly bombarded with information. Technology is changing at a pace that very few can keep up with. Relationships confront us with never-ending challenges. In my life right now, I'm striving to balance marriage, parenting, work, church, health, fitness, aging parents, personal growth and more. I'm currently reading four books and barely making progress in any of them. Thank goodness my wife takes care of paying all the bills! The last time I mowed the lawn it felt like a personal victory!

But I can't say, "Woe is me." My life is no busier, complicated or more demanding than a thousand other leaders I know. Every one of us is struggling to balance life's tensions. What can help us to think clearly and cleanly is simplicity. This truly is a difference maker because in thinking powerfully simple

> *"Every one of us is struggling to balance life's tensions. What can help us to think clearly and cleanly is simplicity."*

thoughts a leader can arrive at powerfully effective solutions.

As I have activated this specific two-minute practice I've discovered three important truths:

1. Simplicity of thought is driven as much by inspiration as by information.

2. Simplicity of thought brings clarity out of chaos.

3. Simplicity of thought always prioritizes people above production.

Admittedly, the summary statement for this two-minute practice sounds like a doctor's prescription: **Take two every day, as often as needed.** In my own experience, that's at least three times a day during the prime working hours. I've come up with a personal reminder that hearkens back to the first major advertising campaign for Dr Pepper—a campaign that was launched nearly a century ago. As corny as it sounds, the Dr Pepper bottling company promoted their product as something to "Enjoy at 10, 2 and 4" as an energy booster. Early Dr Pepper ads featured a clock design with hands pointing to 10, 2 and 4 o'clock. So, I've just adapted that to my own discipline of intensive thinking: Whenever possible, I pause at 10am, 2pm and 4pm and get the energy pick-up not from a sugary drink but from two minutes of super-focused thinking. It generates a lot of great ideas and clear solutions—all with zero calories!

> *Three important truths...*
> *Simplicity of thought...*
> *1. Is driven as much by inspiration as by information.*
> *2. Brings clarity out of chaos.*
> *3. Always prioritizes people above production.*

Practice #3
RELATING
Keep a Leadership Ledger.
Create it wisely. Review it daily. Update it frequently.

Chances are you haven't used the word *ledger* anytime recently. It isn't a common term; and I doubt that you've ever seen it coupled with *leadership*. That is exactly why I chose this word: It is uncommon and unexpected—and for those reasons, much more likely to be memorable.

A ledger is a record of accounts to which debits and credits are posted. A ledger for a mom-and-pop business, for example, would list expenses (debits) and income (credits), and hopefully, a profit rather than a loss. In keeping a simple ledger you can train yourself to see very readily whether things are going positively or negatively, whether you're in the black or in the red.

Now, let's translate this to the concept of a Leadership Ledger. If you're a leader—whether in a large corporation, a small business, a non-profit organization, a church, or some other type of entity—your leadership has one primary focus: People. Yes, leaders lead companies or churches or divisions or projects; but, first and foremost, leaders lead people.

Think of the people whom you lead. Each one has strengths that can be utilized and increased and weaknesses that can be recognized and overcome. As a leader, your goal is to take a positive approach to both. In your Leadership Ledger, the "accounts" are the people under your authority or influence. The "debits" and "credits" are your actions, your efforts to maximize the positives and minimize the negatives in each person. The Leadership Ledger is therefore really more about you than about your team members. It is a record of how you are doing as a leader. When your influence helps someone to employ one of their strengths in an effective or even an extraordinary way, that is a "credit" in your Leadership Ledger. The same goes when you help someone under your leadership to neutralize a personal weakness. But when you fail to exert a positive influence when you could have done so, that's a "debit" in your Leadership Ledger.

Study the people whom you lead. Identify—to the extent that you're able—what their strengths and weaknesses are. Make it a point to connect with each one in ways that are beneficial to them, to the organization, and to you as well. Do all that you can do to foster productive relationships. All too often, too many leaders give into the notion that "I'm here to get the job done" or "It's not important that they like me." That may have been true during the Industrial Age but it won't fly in the Information Age. Your team members must not only be *able* to work with you—they must *want* to work with you and for you. Great leaders create a healthy balance between a sense of community in the team and a sense of accomplishment both corporately and individually. But, practically speaking, how is this done? To find

> *Great leaders create a healthy balance between a sense of community in the team and a sense of accomplishment both corporately and individually.*

the answer I suggest that we look first of all to the greatest leader who ever lived, Jesus Christ.

Jesus enlisted a diverse team of 12 men who were, to most observers, unimpressively common. Among them were a number of commercial fishermen, an anti-Roman zealot, several tradesmen, and one who held perhaps the most despised occupation: Matthew, the tax collector. Let's zero in on him and take a close look at how Jesus called Matthew to a life of discipleship and how he related to him right from the start. This is relevant because the calling of Matthew reveals the very things that a wise leader will keep track of in his or her Leadership Ledger.

The story of Matthew's calling is found in the ninth chapter of the Gospel that bears his name. In just a handful of fascinating verses (Matthew 9:9-13) are seven key truths about relating that are applicable to us as leaders today:

1. Leaders notice people. The Bible says that Jesus "saw a man called Matthew."[1] This was not a passing glance. No, Jesus saw his soul. He looked at him and sensed that Matthew was ready for a new path. He saw not just a tax collector but a man who would one day be a totally-committed apostle. Wise leaders see in their team members not just who they are presently but who they could be potentially. As a leader do you really see the people on your team? Do you look at them with a genuine concern for what they laugh about, cry about and dream about? And do you then lead them accordingly?

> *Wise leaders see their team members not just as who they are presently but as who they could be potentially.*

2. Leaders invite others to join them on a journey. Jesus addressed Matthew directly: He said to him, "Follow me."[2] It was a simple invitation, but it implied a radical change. Jesus was calling Matthew to leave behind the mediocrity of his current existence and become part of a journey toward real significance and true purpose. To be the best leader you can be, you must seize timely opportunities to speak words of challenge. What journey is your team on?

How are you communicating excitement and encouragement to those who are with you on that journey?

3. Leaders inspire positive response. Matthew instantly got up and willingly walked away from his life as a tax collector for Caesar in order to follow Christ. The Bible says "he got up and followed him."[3] Jesus inspired a positive response, which is exactly what an effective leader aims to achieve. Is this how you lead? Do you try to call forth a positive response instead of demanding one? Are you doing your best to inspire and not to interfere?

4. Leaders build strategic relationships. Jesus connected with his new disciple in such a positive way that it opened the door to relationships with people in Matthew's sphere of influence. The Gospel says, "many tax collectors and sinners came and ate with him and his disciples...."[4] Great leaders are open to people and not judgmental towards them. They build bridges to others who may be very different in background and temperament. As a leader, how are you at connecting with people? Do you communicate with your team members out of professional obligation or out of personal desire? Are you willing to cross barriers to build relationships?

5. Leaders build a strong core. In addition to Matthew, Jesus called 11 other men to be his key disciples. There were actually many other disciples, but those 12 men were the core group with whom he spent most of his time and into whom he poured most of his energies. As the ideal leader, he paid special attention to them and he engaged them in amazing experiences and offered them extraordinary opportunities. Do you have a core group who look to you for leadership? It doesn't matter whether they number 12 or just two or three. What matters is whether you're showing that you value them by engaging them in memorable experiences and offering them great opportunities. If you do these things, your core group—whatever its size—will go from strength to strength.

6. Leaders intervene when they have to. When the Pharisees saw Jesus having dinner at Matthew's house with a group of people whom they considered to be socially undesirable, they confronted some of Jesus' disciples and asked, "Why does your teacher eat with tax collectors and sinners?"[5] Jesus overheard the question and came to the aid of his disciples, cutting off the detractors. There are times in leadership when you need to step in and provide relief for those on your team. The Pharisees' confrontation with the disciples could have been a disastrous experience had Jesus not intervened. As a leader do you readily come to the defense of your team members? Are you so tuned-in that you know when to step in and lighten the load for those on your team who are weighed down in some way?

> *There are times in leadership when you need to step in and provide relief for those on your team.*

7. Leaders are insightful problem solvers. Upon hearing the complaint of the Pharisees, Jesus was ready with an answer. Actually, he was ready with a bold statement: "It is not the healthy who need a doctor, but the sick."[6] Then he added, "...go and learn what this means: 'I desire mercy, not sacrifice.' For I have not come to call the righteous, but sinners."[7] Jesus never missed anything. Perhaps the most under-valued skill of great leaders is this ability to see the real issue and speak to it at the right time. That only comes from taking time to listen, to truly listen, to the people on your team. What about you? Are you doing your homework as a leader? Are you aware of the real issues confronting your team? Are you con-stantly improving your craft and honing your skills so you'll know how and when to help solve problems?

So, bearing all these things in mind, let's return to the Leadership Ledger. Remember, the Leadership Ledger keeps account primarily of how you are doing as a leader, not how your team members are doing in their roles. Those team members are the "ac-counts" on your Ledger. As you think about them, ask yourself these questions:

1. What am I seeing in my team members?

2. How am I challenging them?

3. How am I inspiring them?

4. Am I building strategic relationships with them?

5. Do I have a strong core of team members—and am I helping them get stronger?

6. Am I intervening in situations and crises when it is really necessary?

7. Am I offering insightful solutions to those on my team?

These questions frame the structure of your Leadership Ledger. Whether you keep this in the form of a journal or a spreadsheet or running text is totally up to you. Come up with something that works for you and use it as a reference point as you lead from day to day. Sometimes you will want to think long and hard about the people and the questions, but usually just a quick two-minute glance from time to time can make a huge difference in your effectiveness as a leader.

The desired result in any ledger is a positive bottom line. So it is with this key practice. Your "credits" should outnumber your "debits." It's really very simple. And what you will discover is this: Positive leadership is inseparable from positive relationship.

Practice #4
ENLISTING
Look to a Person's Past, Present and Potential.

When hiring, assigning or reviewing, let a person's past inform you, their present instruct you and their potential inspire you.

Genius often comes down to making the complicated simple, but seldom if ever is genius expressed in making the simple complicated. This is a vital lesson for leaders because the natural human inclination is to complicate things. I confess: My default mode is to strive to find 7 Steps, 21 Principles, 10 Keys or some similar list of multiple points. I say to myself, *Brian, there has to be a formula, a method or a system that can be applied to this situation, this problem, this challenge, etc.* And then I think, *If I can just apply these points, sprinkled in with some people skills, then I'll be successful.*

Of course, life and leadership don't usually work out that way. Simplicity, not complexity, is what really makes the difference most of the time—and that is especially true in identifying and enlisting the right people and leading them in the right way. In my quarter of a century as a leader and a student of leadership, I have learned (often the hard way) that the best approach to people is the simple, direct route, not the circuitous path. And, parallel to that thought, the best way to enlist the right people is simply, directly and with clear recognition of the facts about them. To do this most effectively, the leader must try not to impose personal traits or tendencies on the process. Wise leaders don't seek out people who are just like them. If someone doesn't fit into your mold, that is probably a very good thing. So-called "mavericks" in particular can take an organization into new areas of growth and influence.

When I use the term *enlistment* I'm not limiting that to hiring someone. Enlistment certainly includes

> *Wise leaders don't seek out people who are just like them. If someone doesn't fit your mold, that is probably a very good thing.*

hiring (and the process before the hire takes place), but it is much broader. Enlistment happens constantly as leaders recruit for specific positions, make specific assignments and do specific reviews before determining promotions. The two-minute practice I developed for this particular discipline is stated very simply: ***Look to a Person's Past, Present and Potential.*** More specifically, determine whether their present is living up to their past and whether they truly have the potential to succeed in the job or assignment or project being considered. For a brand-new hire, I have even asked a prospective team member: "In terms of work, how does the person you are today compare to the person you've been in the past and the person you want to be in the future?" The answers (if truthful) can be very revealing.

A word of caution to older leaders: If you view younger people as too inexperienced, too irresponsible or too incapable of growth into leadership, you may do so at your own peril. The hard truth is that revolutionary ideas don't usually come from people past the age of 45. How does this relate to enlistment? It's a reminder to not allow a person's inexperience to prevent them from gaining experience and succeeding in it. Look to the potential. Remember the example of Jesus? He enlisted a group of young men and poured his life into training them, putting up with them and enduring them, all the while seeing ahead to what they would become. I'm not Jesus and neither are you; but as leaders we can certainly learn a thing or two from his example when it comes to enlistment.

Now, at the risk of comparing people to animals...I'm going to compare people to animals. Specifically, horses. (Stay with me here.) This comparison actually began when I was trying to deal with some particularly challenging individuals. If you've been a leader even for a short time you undoubtedly know what I mean by *challenging*. Whether you're a leader in a church, a company, a sports team or a non-profit organization, you will at some time or another be called on to lead people who are talented but difficult. They cause friction. They provoke frustration. They upset other people. They are a pain in

> *"You will at some time or another be called on to lead people who are talented but difficult."*

the rear. Often, they resist being led. So, how do you lead them? Someone shared with me an analogy that helps to answer that question.

Before I get to the analogy, let me interject that there's a difference between a *frustrating* person and one who is *insubordinate*. Insubordination or defiance can never be tolerated and must be dealt with swiftly. Frustration is a different matter entirely and individuals who cause it should be handled in a different manner.

Back to the analogy: People are like horses. (When I blogged about this subject some time ago, I wrote that frustrating people are like horses. Since writing that I have realized that all people are like horses because all people at some time or another can be frustrating!) Let me paint a picture for you of six different types of horses representing six different personalities or temperaments in the workplace: Thoroughbreds, Clydesdales, Plow Horses, Quarter Horses, Miniatures and Tennessee Walkers. (And, lest you think that I've forgotten that this chapter is about enlisting, I assure you I haven't.)

THOROUGHBREDS

First, the **Thoroughbreds**—the race horses of your organization. When thoroughbreds are in their stalls before a race, they eat other horses' food. They buck and snarl when they are led to the track. They kick over buckets. They resist getting into the chutes. They seem constantly disgruntled. But when the gates open and the race starts, they easily out-perform all other types of horses.

In an organizational setting, the Thoroughbreds are those whose expense reports inevitably have something incorrect, who fail to turn in reports on time, who color outside the lines, who often don't play well with others. But despite all that—they are top performers. In many companies, the Thorough-

> *With Thoroughbreds...make sure you give them a track to run on...your focus must be on minimizing their weaknesses and removing obstacles that may slow them down and hinder their success.*

breds are the top-producing individuals in sales and marketing. In a church setting, the Thoroughbred might be the senior pastor, the worship leader or even the staff member who is socially dysfunctional with individuals or small groups but absolutely captivating in front of large crowds. Thoroughbreds need guidelines, not fiercely enforced rules. When enlisting Thoroughbreds make sure you give them a track to run on. Your objective is not to help them see their strengths (they won't have any problem doing that); rather, your focus must be on minimizing their weaknesses and removing obstacles that may slow them down and hinder their success.

CLYDESDALES

Clydesdales are majestic and attractive. If you were to put them in a race, they would look impressive going to the gate. But they wouldn't burst out like a Thoroughbred; instead, a Clydesdale would likely step out a few steps and pause as if to say, "Hey, you down there...look at me." Clydesdales are built for endurance, not for speed. They can carry a heavier load and hold up under greater pressures.

Clydesdales often lack rudimentary people skills and can be blunt, perhaps even suggesting that others' work is below par, no matter how much the others have produced. They may stress their own superiority by emphasizing what others are not doing—with a 10-page PowerPoint to prove it. They may seem haughty, but their strength and teamwork are legendary. They don't always "race" well, but they

> *[Clydesdales] don't always 'race' well, but they can carry an organization to greater success.*

can carry an organization to greater success. Clydesdales on your team are meant to be in roles that demand patient endurance and quality consciousness. Look closely at their history in comparison with their current performance to lead them most effectively.

PLOW HORSES

Plow Horses are not fast but they are productive. They consistently pull more than their weight; but they can be doggedly stubborn and sometimes downright irritating. Hollywood doesn't make movies about Plow Horses. They will never perform like the Thoroughbreds. They will not impress like the Clydesdales. But every strong organization needs a number of Plow Horses who do what only they can do. The best way to lead them is to honor them. Don't take them for granted, which is so easy to let happen.

> *The best way to lead [Plow Horses] is to honor them. Don't take them for granted, which is easy to let happen.*

QUARTER HORSES

In the animal kingdom, the **Quarter Horse** is called a Quarter Horse because of its exceptional ability to sprint a quarter of a mile or less. Some have been clocked at speeds up to 55 miles per hour! A Quarter Horse is a born performer, able and agile and capable of intricate maneuvers. In the long run, a Quarter Horse is no match for a Thoroughbred; but in a sprint, it usually isn't a contest. The Quarter Horses in your organization are the people built for speed but not necessarily for the pounding endurance required for a long race. In other words, they can take on projects of shorter scope but higher intensity and perform in an extraordinary way. Quarter Horse members are essential to team balance, especially in a larger organization, because they provide bursts of power that give

> *[Quarter Horses] can take on projects of shorter scope but higher intensity and perform in an extraordinary way.*

impetus to jobs that simply have to be done and done well. The rest of the time they are like Plow Horses, doing their job and holding their own until circumstances call for a great output of energy.

MINIATURES

The **Miniature Horse**, believe it or not, is a very common breed. Although small in size, they are not ponies but full horses. They come in many variations of color and appearance. Their human equivalents—the Miniatures of the workplace—can be charming and engaging, but they often have a tendency to let their limitations in aptitude or ability negatively affect their production. They are prone to feel put-down or disrespected—even when they aren't being put

The Miniatures of the workplace can be charming and engaging, but they often have a tendency to let their limitations in aptitude or ability negatively affect their production.

down or disrespected! To lead a Miniature on your team you have to show kindness and sensitivity but resist letting them feel sorry for themselves. Deal with a firm hand, express true respect, and a Miniature will make a great effort and produce a great result.

TENNESSEE WALKERS

Then there's the **Tennessee Walker**. They run a bit differently from all the others; sometimes they seem awkward but usually they're quite impressive. The Tennessee Walkers on your team are among the most pleasant people you will ever lead. They have a steady pace and a calm disposition. They hold their heads high, stay focused and remain sure-footed in a crisis. If called upon, they will take the lead on a project, even entering the "show ring" if need be; but

> *If called upon, [Tennessee Walkers] will take the lead on a project...but they're just as happy galloping along with the rest of the team.*

they're just as happy galloping along with the rest of the team. Leading them is simpler than leading just about any other type of worker; but guard against complacency about them and praise them readily.

Do you recognize the Thoroughbreds, Clydesdales, Plow Horses, Quarter Horses, Miniatures and Tennessee Walkers in your organization? Can they be a pain in the rear at times? Of course! But don't let that derail how you enlist them. See them for what they are and do your best to empower them to be what they can be. Make this important two-minute practice a priority in your leadership. And whether you're hiring for a new position, making an assignment on a big project or doing a review, recognize that you need all types of people and the task at hand may be better handled by a Plow Horse than by a Thoroughbred. Look to the track record. Look to the current performance. And look very honestly at what that person's potential truly is—never assuming that they know it themselves, because you may see something they will never see. A spotty track record discourages many a team member; but it can be overcome with solid, day-to-day performance; and that very fact may help in determining that a big assignment or a promotion is in order.

Take a good look at your team. When hiring, assigning or reviewing, let a person's past inform you, their present instruct you and their potential inspire you.

> *"When hiring, assigning or reviewing, let a person's past inform you, their present instruct you and their potential inspire you."*

Practice #5
POSITIONING
Align the Elements.

Strategically position every key project
with key preparations and key people.

I don't play chess. But I do know how the game is played and I'm impressed by those who play it well. It has occurred to me on more than one occasion that successful leaders are like winning chess players: they think ahead and make decisive moves that lead to other decisive moves and—more often than not—to a positive outcome. They are masters in the art of strategic positioning.

Effective leaders first learn the vital discipline of positioning on a personal level. When I began to write this chapter I recalled a fascinating article about famed Hollywood producer and director Dino De Laurentiis.[1] Over his seven-decade career in the movie business, De Laurentiis produced more than 500 films, was nominated for Academy Awards over 30 times and won two Oscars. In reading the tribute to his life I gleaned so much about his work ethic. In fact, I counted seven decisive factors that positioned him for long-term success. Let me express each one in the form of a directive to leaders and prospective leaders:

1. Seize the best opportunities to make moves toward your dream. As a 17-year-old, De Laurentiis worked as a movie extra while at the same time pursuing his studies at the Centro Sperimentale di Cinematografia in Rome. He snapped up every chance to better position himself to reach his ultimate goals.

2. Develop multiple skills within your discipline. By the time he turned 20, De Laurentiis had worked in the movie business as a general laborer, prop man, cashier, assistant director and unit production manager. Gaining knowledge and experience in multiple areas of his craft provided the young Dino with strategic advantages over others who were older but more limited.

3. Grow in confidence. The more he learned, the more De Laurentiis improved and the more his confidence was heightened. He recognized, even as a young man, that he was positioning himself to succeed in the rough-and-tumble motion picture industry.

4. Develop resourcing strategies. By making the right moves, honing his know-how and constantly adding to his expertise, De Laurentiis was able to secure financial backing and launch his own film production company. Personal positioning led to financial positioning.

5. Demonstrate true innovation. De Laurentiis was one of the first in his field to produce films set among the under-privileged working class. He recognized that his humble beginnings gave him a valuable perspective; he then used that perspective to depict life's raw realities and win a growing audience of fans.

6. Go for big ideas. In his acclaimed movie, *War and Peace*, De Laurentiis was among the first to film grand-scale battle scenes. He wasn't afraid to go big. He knew that positioning typically involves small, incremental moves; but he also knew that leaders must sometimes go big to set the stage for greater success.

7. Identify top talent. In his successful 1976 remake of *King Kong*, De Laurentiis discovered the now-famous actress Jessica Lange. She was only one of many actors to whom he provided a breakthrough moment. Throughout his career he demonstrated that a key element of leadership is the positioning of the right people in the right way and in the right places.

Wise positioning is crucial to wise leadership. Coaches and managers of great sports teams know that the positioning of players can spell the difference between victory and defeat. Corporate leaders know that the right man or woman in the right slot can transform an entire organization...or cause irreparable damage. Pastors, too, can attest to the effects—positive and negative—of strategic positioning in a church's leadership structure.

> *The right man or woman in the right slot can transform an entire organization...or cause irreparable damage.*

When I first began writing this chapter the key word I chose for this practice was *preparation*. However, the more I got into it, the more I realized that I was actually describing *positioning* for success, not *preparing* for it. I then reworded the practice itself to state: **Align the Elements: Strategically position every key project with key preparations and key people.** I cannot overstate the importance of this because strategic positioning leads to strategic performance—personally and corporately.

On September 11, 2001, Colonel Mark Tillman was the lead pilot of Air Force One. The day began uneventfully, but a crisis of historic proportions was about to strike the nation, and Col. Tillman was about to play a key role in an unprecedented drama. He was the right man, positioned in the right place, ready to face the challenge head-on. Recalling that red-letter day he said, "There are all kinds of plans to keep the president safe...even in the event of a nuclear attack.... I knew exactly what to do with the president and where to take him to keep him safe."[2] But that wasn't all he was prepared to do. Immediately after the attacks, while President Bush was being rushed back to the airport, Tillman personally double-checked the identity of everyone on board Air Force One, restricted the number of officials allowed to get back on the plane, posted an extra security officer outside the cockpit and, once the President was back on board, took off at once. He was positioned to fly the leader of the free world to the most secure place possible and was bold enough to advise President Bush not to return to Washington. He explained in a recent interview, "One of the concerns was that Washington was where the terrorists would expect us to run to if something happened. My plan was not to get back to Washington right away."[3] Col. Tillman recommended Barksdale Air Force Base just outside Shreveport, Louisiana, knowing it to be a rock-solid, secure location.

Says Col. Tillman, "I wasn't thinking about the American people at the time, or who had been killed or who had been injured. My goal was to keep the President safe and to do my job. It wasn't until I landed back at Andrews and went back to my office that I realized exactly what we'd done that day and how much we still had to do."[4] Tillman went on to fly Air Force One for eight more years, including 49 foreign trips and flights to 49 of the 50 states. He also piloted Air Force One back to Texas after President Bush left office. Tillman, who then retired from the service, went out on top. When asked about his parting thoughts, he explained how it had all started for him as a pre-med student at Tulane University. He noticed that a classmate was in uniform so he asked why and learned about the R.O.T.C. program. Discovering that the U.S. Air Force would pay his tuition, he signed up. As his superiors put him through the rigors of testing, Tillman learned that he was more naturally inclined toward engineering and aviation. His leaders positioned him, and he in turn pursued one opportunity after another, consistently positioning himself for ever-increasing success in a very demanding world.

Now, let's take a closer look at this key two-minute practice. What exactly does it mean to strategically position every key project with key preparations and key people? It means to approach your projects as if you were studying a chessboard. In life and in leadership there will always be a number of opposing pieces on the other side of the board or perhaps already in your territory. How can you strategically position your people and your resources to neutralize and eliminate that opposition? What moves will enable you to sustain momentum? What sacrifices need to be made to ensure ultimate victory? It is unfortunate but necessary to lose pawns or rooks or even a knight in order to win. Col. Mark Tillman wasn't afraid to tell some VIPs, "Sorry, but you can't get back on the plane." They were offended, but he didn't care because he was doing his best to strategically position for the next leg in the most important

> *To strategically position every key project with key preparations and key people...means to approach your projects as if you were studying a chessboard.*

journey he had ever undertaken. In the chess game of leadership, positioning isn't always popular—but it is always necessary.

Strategic positioning demands that you look at key projects in terms of the best ways to ensure a win:

Perhaps the person who could most effectively handle a particular assignment is an unlikely choice. But if you're convinced that it would be a good move, don't be unduly swayed by what others think.

Perhaps the job calls for a new vendor, not the one you would typically go to...and perhaps in giving a new provider a chance you will open up a whole new relationship with a more positive financial outcome.

Perhaps that class at church would be totally revitalized by team teaching vs. a one-man band.

And perhaps you're already thinking about all kinds of possible strategic moves that could make a positive difference for yourself, your team or your organization. Successful positioning focuses on momentum, not on obstacles. Successful positioning is open to change, not resistant to it. Successful positioning maximizes people and resources as it minimizes or neutralizes resistance.

My wife and daughter are fascinated by the Amish people so I surprised them with a trip to historic Lancaster County, Pennsylvania. I booked a room for us at a local B&B, The Smithton Inn, operated by Innkeeper Rebecca Gallagher. From the moment I made the call, Rebecca and the Smithton team strategically positioned our family for an extraordinary experience. After I made the reservation there was immediate follow up online and by mail as well. A beautiful package of materials arrived in our mailbox that same week. It made us anticipate the visit with even more excitement. When we arrived, we were warmly greeted and were told about the best places to eat and the best attractions and were provided easy-to-use maps to get us there. Then there were the special touches. After we mentioned how much we enjoyed the lovely fireplace in our suite, we returned to the room each day to find a log fire already burning. And perhaps the best part of the trip was when Rebecca asked our daughter if she wanted to help her in the kitchen as she prepared our breakfast. That simple invitation captured the hearts of both my daughter and my wife and made for an unforgettable memory. I think that it all came so naturally for Rebecca but she showed me in an unmistakable way how leaders are to take the initiative in a relationship. Without a doubt, she strategically positioned us for a return visit to the Smithton Inn.

Let me take you back to the example of Dino De Laurentiis and ask several questions derived from his life experience. These are relevant, of course, because I'm convinced that De Laurentiis was a master of this two-minute practice of strategic positioning.

Are you seizing the opportunities to make decisive moves toward your personal or corporate dreams?

Are you continuing to gain knowledge and experience in multiple areas of your profession or field?

Are you growing in confidence because you're growing in experience?

Are you developing ways to resource the fulfillment of your dream?

Are you positioning yourself with new, innovative ways to exercise your leadership?

Are you willing and able to position in a big way for big moves?

Are you keeping an eye out for talented people to enlist and invest in?

Answer these questions honestly (and frequently) and you will advance your leadership definitively and perhaps even monumentally.

Practice #6
COMMUNICATING
Communicate Expectations, Directions and Commendations.

Communicate expectations before the fact.
Communicate directions within the bounds.
Communicate commendation without hesitation.

On a brisk December day, I walked into my local Starbucks and greeted the person behind the counter with a joyous "Merry Christmas!" He responded, "Right back at you." I thought, *Right back at you? What's with that?* Returning the next day, I once again said "Merry Christmas!" The response: "Thanks. You too." I did the same for two more days, each time getting in reply a weak "Thank You." Finally, on the fifth day, my persistence paid off. A new person behind the counter, a cheerful middle-aged woman, replied, "Merry Christmas to you, too!" At last, a normal, non-PC answer from someone who was probably disregarding the company's attempts to not "offend" anyone with "religious" language!

Over the next six months, that very pleasant lady served me and my family in an exemplary way. Every time we ordered she remembered our personal preferences without fail. We told her about our family and she told us about hers. Sadly, her marriage was crumbling and one day we learned that she was getting a divorce and would be moving back to her hometown. My wife and I did our best to encourage her, and—strange as it seems—that opportunity to minister to her could be traced back to a persistence in communicating a simple greeting: "Merry Christmas!"

That experience prompted me to start thinking in some new ways about the relationship between leadership and communication. In time, I arrived at three essential elements of a key *2-Minute Leader* practice: ***Communicate expectations before the fact. Communicate directions within the bounds. Communicate commendation without hesitation.*** Let me begin to unpack these keys by explaining more about the lessons learned in my Christmas-time Starbucks encounters. There were seven that stand out:

1. Leaders must communicate in realm of reality. Regardless of your religious beliefs, December

25th is Christmas Day and the month of December is the Christmas season. Leaders aren't afraid to talk about what is real and what it means.

2. Leaders dispense hope. The Christmas season is a time of hope, possibilities and new beginnings. The words "Merry Christmas" communicate hope-filled promise. But hope is not limited to a specific season; and the more I thought about it, the more I realized the role I play as a leader—every day of every season—in dispensing hope to my team members, to my clients, to everyone in the sphere of my influence.

3. Leaders are contagious communicators. "Merry Christmas" is a simple, two-word proclamation. Yet those words have the power to spread a contagion of joy. Others can catch it and spread it to even more people. When I communicate in my role as a leader—regardless of the person or the audience I'm

> *When I communicate in my role as a leader...I have the capacity to deliver a contagious message.*

addressing—I have the capacity to deliver a contagious message (and I'm referring not just to the "Merry Christmas" message). If my communication is positive, the effect will in most cases be positive as well. However, if my communication is negative, I can bring people down in attitude and perspective.

4. Leaders stay true to their character. I am unashamedly a follower of Jesus Christ. My highest aspiration is that his character be reflected in my character. Because of his importance in my life, I am never going to opt for "Happy Holidays" or "Season's Greetings" when I can say, loud and clear, "Merry Christmas!" Enough said on that point.

5. Leaders persist. It took a bull-headed determination to keep going back to Starbucks day after day insistent on sharing a simple greeting of goodwill. I was not going to take "No" for an answer. I wasn't going to stop until someone said "Merry Christmas" back to me. When you communicate as a leader, be certain of yourself and don't allow negative responses to alter your approach or derail your intentions.

> *Your words have power so use them with wisdom and sensitivity.*

6. Leaders build bridges. Those two words— "Merry Christmas"—created an opportunity to establish a connection with someone who was hurting and in need of friendship. Your words have that same power, so use them with wisdom and sensitivity.

7. Leaders see the bigger picture. My Starbucks experience wasn't about me or my communication. I had to get beyond the irritation of a "neutral" response and remind myself that Christmas is transcendent. It is about Jesus; and every opportunity to say "Merry Christmas" is a golden moment to honor the One who gives us life itself. Year-round, the wise leader communicates with the bigger picture in mind.

Now, let's return to that triply-important *2-Minute Leader* practice: ***Communicate expectations before the fact. Communicate directions within the bounds. Communicate commendation without hesitation.*** Some thoughts on each one:

71

Communicate expectations before the fact.

What does it mean to communicate expectations before the fact? It means to let people know ahead of time what you expect of them in a job or a project or a meeting or an initiative. Remember how maddening it was as a kid when you were disciplined for breaking a rule that you didn't even know was a rule? That was a failure of parenting. The workplace equivalent is a failure of leadership—brought about by leaders who keep expectations to themselves and for some reason don't let others know about those expectations until they aren't met! As a leader, when I make an assignment I can't make the assumption that my team member can read my mind and know what I anticipate as the desired results. I must always communicate my expectations before the fact, not afterwards.

> *I can't make the assumption that my team member can read my mind and know what I anticipate as the desired results.*

Communicate directions within the bounds.

Communicating directions within the bounds is a bit more complex. As a leader you have to know what the boundaries are, and that is not always apparent. When I give directions to someone, I have to be mindful to not talk down to them, to not talk past them, and to not talk above them. All of those are examples of communicating outside the bounds. They show condescension, indifference or superiority. To communicate within the bounds is to demonstrate respect, to express clarity and to show humility. If you give directions and then proceed to tell the recipient how to do his or her job, you've gone outside the bounds. Unless the person is in training you have to allow them to do their job, even if their approach is different from yours.

The worst violations come from leaders who are bullies. Bullying is generating a lot of discussion these days. The problem is not a new phenomenon. It has always existed and it is all too prevalent among leaders at all levels in all types of organizations and companies. I have no patience with leaders who are

> *To communicate within the bounds is to demonstrate respect, to express clarity and to show humility.*

bullies, and one day I was prompted to write a blog post that was actually a rant about bullies. I asked the question: Are you a bully? I answered the question by listing the telltale characteristics:

1. Bullies lead by fear.

2. Bullies degrade, insult and "encourage" or "train" their team members publicly.

3. Bullies make others feel intellectually weak.

4. Bullies are quick to say, "You are easily replaceable."

5. Bullies consistently focus on what others are not rather than what they are.

6. Bullies (who are men) do not respect women and often view them as objects.

7. Bullies talk incessantly about their personal accomplishments.

8. Bullies are narcissistic.

9. Bullies often make statements such as, "You're lucky to have a job in this economy."

10. Bullies have minimal relational intelligence.

If you are in the unfortunate position of serving under a bully, here is what you need to know. Your boss is going to fail. A bullying leadership style is not sustainable. The diminished sense of loyalty, low morale and frequent (and sometimes heated) conflicts will eventually undermine everything. The team will not go the extra mile when a bully is in charge. The rate of turnover will be high, forcing increased time on training and development of replacements rather than advancing the mission and vision of the organization. Customers or clients (or church mem-

The team will not go the extra mile when a bully is in charge.

bers) will look for other options. Goals will go unmet as the bully leader loses influence and, ultimately, loses his or her job.

That's the silver lining. Bullies will eventually get what's due them. If you're a bully, here is a note to you: Stop communicating outside the acceptable bounds. Your leadership style may get people to fall in line; but don't confuse compliance with agreement. Your abrasiveness causes unnecessary stress, and you are not sustainable. If others keep their heads low, do their jobs, and do their best to stay out of your way, you will one day be gone—and the riddance will be good.

The sad thing is, some would have fought hell with a water pistol for you. Some would have gone the extra mile and served you with everything they had. But you had to be a bully and because of that decision, you will pay the price. Of course, it's not too late to change. Repent and start serving your team. If you're a bully, you are ultimately out of options, whether you know it or not.

Sorry, but I felt that was worth repeating—and a good reminder to all of us as leaders to communicate directions within the bounds: the bounds of respect, responsibility and humility.

Communicate commendation without hesitation.

The third element of this *2-Minute Leader* practice—communicating commendation without hesitation—is a tough one for many leaders to master. You may be good at clarifying expectations and excellent at staying within the bounds; but if you are resistant to give praise when praise is due, your standing as a leader will suffer. If someone on your team has gone above and beyond the call of duty or worked with exceptional diligence, then commendation should be given. "But they're just doing their jobs!" some leaders will argue, as if that's a reason not to show recognition. Such an attitude is foolish and results in undermining one's own leadership.

> "*If you are resistant to give praise... your standing as a leader will suffer.*"

In my observation of hundreds of organizations, the leaders who are best at communicating commendation without hesitation are the leaders who are good listeners. Listening is not merely an absence of words while someone else is talking. It is deeper than not interrupting. Listening is a core habit of servant leadership. A leader who listens well communicates care for others, concern for the feelings of others, interest in the thoughts of others and a desire to learn from others. This, in turn, creates a heart disposition toward giving praise where praise is due.

Are you a good communicator? I'm not asking whether you're a good public speaker or a superb salesman. To determine whether or not you're a good communicator you have to go deeper. And to be the best you can be, you would be wise to remember this key *2-Minute Leader* practice: Communicate expectations before the fact. Communicate directions within the bounds. Communicate commendation without hesitation. It's actually very simple. But, ironically, it's also very hard.

Practice #7
EXECUTING
Take AIM.

Activate your plan.
Integrate your resources.
Mobilize your team.

It was late, very late. I had worked far too long that day and turned on the TV for a few moments of mindless entertainment. Zipping through the program guide on my cable line-up I saw what promised to be the most inane possibility: Professional Wrestling. I liked it as a kid…why not give it a chance now? I clicked the station and suddenly the screen was filled with the image of a menacing wrestler in hideous trunks. The announcer's voice boomed, "Randy Orton is the apex predator!"

"Apex predator?" I said out loud. The silliness on-screen ensued but I was lost in thought already, fixated on one word: *Apex*. Not a term that I use every day (not at that time, at least). I knew its meaning and I liked its sound: Apex—the highest point. It got me to thinking about leadership (of course). As the TV blared on, my mind was racing. A new question was driving my thoughts: *What makes an Apex Leader?* Over the next few days I couldn't let go of that question and I began making a list of what I now call the qualities of an Apex Leader. I began taking special notice whenever I heard a statement that seemed to fit the Apex category...

"He's at the top of his game."

"It was the pinnacle of achievement."

"She was the ultimate performer."

In a relatively short time I had compiled a long list of qualities and numerous examples of Apex accomplishment. Remembering to keep it simple, I distilled all of those qualities into the acronym AIM—for Activate, Integrate and Mobilize. More specifically: A *2-Minute Leader* (who is also, ideally, an Apex Leader) takes AIM by **A**ctivating a plan, **I**ntegrating resources and **M**obilizing people.

It's all about coordinated execution—putting a strategy into motion, pulling essentials together and leading a team forward. To make it happen, and to keep it happening, several qualities are key, but three stand out: A visionary heart, a multi-faceted mind and a generous spirit. In fact, these became the top three on my list of Apex Leader Qualities. Let's take a closer look at each one:

A Visionary Heart. King David of Israel, one of the greatest leaders in world history, ruled his nation for over 40 years. David's final act of leadership, the apex of his life, was to issue the challenge to construct the Temple—a monumental edifice that would bear not his name but that of his son, Solomon. The Old Testament book of First Chronicles, chapters 28-29, gives us a sense of what made him such a great leader. It all started with vision. David said, "I had it in my heart to build...."[1] He was compelled by a visionary heart that enabled him to see what did not yet exist.

King David saw the future and accepted the reality of great things in which he would not be personally

> *David was compelled by a visionary heart that enabled him to see what did not yet exist.*

involved. He was an Apex Leader whose sight was not restricted by selfish motives and who willingly did all that he could do in his time. There's a Bible verse that I love that says simply, "David...served God's purpose in his own generation...."[2] We can only serve God in the generation in which we live, but with a visionary heart we can look beyond our times and ourselves and act on behalf of those who come after us. That's the kind of leader I want to be: one who acts not just for himself but for his children and grandchildren and generations to come.

A Multi-Faceted Mind. We talk a lot these days about multi-tasking—doing several things simultaneously. I know of a man who can actually carry on two phone conversations at the same time, with a separate phone on each ear, and with a constant switching on and off of the mute buttons as he talks to two different people! That is taking multi-tasking to an extreme; but, the fact is, effective leaders are effective multi-taskers. A person who has difficulty working concurrently on numerous projects, communicating with numerous people and balancing numerous priorities is highly unlikely to be a good leader. I don't know of a single leader who focuses on only one thing at a time to the exclusion of all other things (with the exception of those rare times when a challenge arises and demands full and sole attention).

King David, the consummate leader of his generation, was a multi-tasker. His visionary heart was beating in sync with his multi-faceted mind. Not only did he envision the future, he also saw what was necessary to get there. David summoned all the officials of Israel to a special assembly in the nation's capital, Jerusalem. He called in all the tribal leaders, all the military commanders and all the governmental authorities; and to that great gathering he announced, "I had it in my heart to build a house as a place of rest for the ark of the covenant of the Lord, for the

> *King David, the consummate leader of his generation, was a multi-tasker. His visionary heart was beating in sync with his multi-faceted mind.*

footstool of our God...."[3] Then David added, "and I made plans to build it."[4] Next, he laid out the details: The builder would be David's son, Solomon, who would reign as king after his father's death. David explained that Solomon was God's chosen one for a history-making building project; and—in the presence of the assembly—David charged Solomon to follow God's leading and serve the Lord with whole-hearted devotion and a willing mind. David then presented Solomon with the plans for the temple and its surrounding courts—the plans that God's Spirit had put in his mind. "All this," David said, "I have in writing as a result of the Lord's hand on me, and he enabled me to understand all the details of the plan."[5]

Next, King David revealed the third vital quality:

A Generous Spirit. David said to everyone: "With all my resources I have provided for the temple of my God—gold for the gold work, silver for the silver, bronze for the bronze, iron for the iron and wood for the wood, as well as onyx for the settings, turquoise, stones of various colors, and all kinds of fine stone and marble—all of these in large quantities.

Besides, in my devotion to the temple of my God I now give my personal treasures of gold and silver for the temple of my God, over and above everything I have provided for this holy temple."[6] David led by casting the vision and marshalling the team and finally by practicing extreme generosity—giving above and beyond in a way that set the example for others to follow. He challenged them: "Now, who is willing to consecrate themselves to the Lord today?"[7] The question resonated and the people responded: "Then the leaders of families, the officers of the tribes of Israel, the commanders of thousands and commanders of hundreds, and the officials in charge of the king's work gave willingly. They gave toward the work on the temple of God five thousand talents and ten thousand darics of gold, ten thousand talents of silver, eighteen thousand talents of bronze and a hun-

> *"David led by casting the vision and marshalling the team and finally by practicing extreme generosity...."*

dred thousand talents of iron. Anyone who had precious stones gave them to the treasury of the temple of the Lord...."[8] David's apex generosity inspired all the other leaders to be generous, and their generosity in turn stirred the entire nation: "The people rejoiced at the willing response of their leaders, for they had given freely and wholeheartedly to the Lord."[9]

> *David's generosity inspired all the other leaders to be generous, and their generosity in turn stirred the nation.*

It's a massive leap, but let's jump from King David of ancient Israel to José Mourinho of modern-day Portugal. Perhaps you're wondering, *Who in the world is José Mourinho?* Well, according to *Sports Illustrated*, he is "the best coach in any sport, anywhere." Not Bill Belichick. Not Phil Jackson. Not Tony La Russa. Not Pat Summitt. Nope, none of those very gifted leaders. José Mourinho wins the award. Why? Because in the world's biggest sport—soccer—José Mourinho has led his teams to such heights of success that his players have given him the nickname, "The Special One."[10]

José Mourinho exemplifies the *2-Minute Leader* practice that is the subject of this chapter: He takes AIM every day. He activates his plan. He integrates his resources. He mobilizes his team. Mourinho's plan is multi-dimensional and tailored to fit a variety of personalities, opponents and ever-shifting situations. He is a student not just of sports, but also of business, psychology and team dynamics. In a recent interview he observed, "A football coach who only understands football cannot be a great coach."[11] Mourinho integrates his key resources—his players— by relating to each one in a different way, relative to their temperament, demeanor, culture and language. He speaks five languages fluently and uses each one to his advantage. But when speaking to the entire team he always addresses them in the language of the home nation. In competition, Mourinho mobilizes his team by deftly coaching his players to handle the transitions from offense to defense. He explains, "You must have a great balance. That's why I believe in having players with the tactical culture to analyze the game. All of them have to think the same thing at the same time."[12] Time after time, year after year, they do think the same thing at the same time; and in the process they win time after time, year after year. In great measure, the victories result not just from the players on the field but also from their Apex Leader on the sidelines.

What about you? Are you taking AIM? Are you activating your plan every day? Are you integrating the resources at hand? Are you mobilizing your team for maximum effectiveness? Answering these questions affirmatively implies that you have a plan, that you know your resources and that you are well connected to your team. These are the prerequisites. Implicit in this is some degree of complexity because as a leader you may very well have parallel plans, a variety of resources and even multiple teams. My pastor, for example, has plans for his preaching ministry, his administrative role, his general responsibilities to the church and his specific responsibilities to several constituencies within the church. He draws from resources in the congregation and beyond the congregation. He mobilizes several teams—elders, staff, lay leaders and more. For him—and perhaps for you, as well—taking AIM is not a one-time, one-track exercise but an ongoing challenge on multiple platforms. But taking AIM is crucial to hitting targets and achieving goals.

> *Taking AIM is not a one-time, one-track exercise but an ongoing challenge on multiple platforms.*

On Sunday evenings our family often attends Passion City Church in Atlanta—certainly one of the world's most unusual churches. PCC's lead pastor, Louie Giglio, is a remarkably gifted communicator of God's Word. And the church's worship leader is no slouch. He is Chris Tomlin, the most influential composer and the top male vocalist in Christian music. At a recent service I bought a copy of Tomlin's album, *And If Our God Is For Us*. Included was a bonus DVD that I watched with great interest. I was struck especially by one statement by Chris: "We're not looking for just the next hit that's going to last for three months. We want something that's going to last...[something] that becomes kind of a soundtrack in [people's] lives." The entire DVD was to me a powerhouse example of Apex Leadership being exercised by a man who is truly taking AIM every day... taking AIM by seeking long-term significance above short-term success...taking AIM by seeking a message that transcends time...and taking AIM by seeking God's glory above personal acclaim.

So, my challenge to you is simple: Master this *2-Minute Leader* practice. Take AIM: Activate your plan. Integrate your resources. Mobilize your team. And if you do so with a visionary heart, a multifaceted mind and a generous spirit, your life will be enriched in ways beyond measure.

Practice #8
ADJUSTING
Check Your Bearings and Adjust as Needed.
Stay alert to changing conditions and ready to make course corrections.

I had to work on Memorial Day. Frankly, I wasn't happy about it, and I certainly hadn't looked forward to it; but it was something I simply had to do. A large denomination was having its annual convention and I was needed to man our company's booth in the exhibit hall.

I had represented our firm on many occasions at many conventions, so I had learned that the best fruit is often found at the end of the branch. In other words, the best opportunities come late in the day or when I am physically worn out. And seldom is the branch within easy reach. It takes a special effort. So, I knew from experience that if I just carried out my assignment with diligence and excellence, something good could very possibly happen. And that day it did.

At nearly 6:00 p.m., just before closing time, I met the man who is arguably the most successful church builder in America. He was intelligent, had a very kind manner, and had a portfolio that wowed me. But what resonated most with me during our conversation was what he said when I asked how he first got involved in building churches.

He explained that many years ago he was serving as pastor of a church whose building was destroyed when a bad thermocouple caused a massive explosion. The news arrived in an urgent phone call with a terse message: "Pastor, the church's furnace just blew up." Fortunately, the building was unoccupied and no one was hurt; but the entire facility would have to be rebuilt. In an instant, the conditions of his pastorate had changed abruptly and dramatically, and he would have to make a radical course correction. He had comfortably worn the hat of pastor but now he was called on to put on another hat: that of general contractor.

What seemed at first to be a great inconvenience was actually a remarkable opportunity because he turned out to be a very accomplished builder. Other churches began asking for his help and before he knew it, he was working on projects for eight other congregations! He was faced with another set of unexpected circumstances. Conditions had changed once again and he felt strongly the need for another course correction. God was calling him to make a major adjustment—from serving one church to serving many.

As I listened to this man's fascinating story, several questions began to surface in my mind...

Is there a "thermocouple" going bad today that I don't even know about that could result in re-directing and changing my life in a positive way?

Is there some kind of "furnace" about to blow up?

Is there somebody whose life was just racked by an explosion and needs my help?

"What seemed at first to be a great inconvenience was actually a remarkable opportunity because he turned out to be a very accomplished builder."

Is there something going on, nearby or perhaps far away, that is about to unleash the possibility of significant blessings in my life?

Is there something going on with my team members that I haven't noticed? Is there an undercurrent of complaints or concerns?

I have discovered that implementing the two-minute practice of checking my bearings and adjusting as needed is actually one of the harder practices because it often calls for in-depth attention and focus on something I may have been avoiding or had totally missed beforehand. As leaders, we don't know what's coming next and we never have all the information. Success is in great measure determined by things we can control—our own sweat equity, our own preparation, our own determination. However, success also comes through discernment—being aware of and being open to new opportunities and seeming "inconveniences." It is the "chance" meeting, the new book someone recommended, the overheard remark, the random suggestion or the unexpected phone call that when properly leveraged

> *Success...comes through discernment — being aware of and being open to new opportunities and seeming inconveniences.*

can take your life or your organization to the next level.

The enemies of inconvenient opportunity are marginalization and over-extension. If we are too busy to listen, too closed to new input and too resistant to adjustment, our growth will be limited. If we don't have the proper margin in our schedule or thinking, we will never be able to identify and take advantage of new opportunities.

Since I have (for better or for worse) a steady-as-he-goes personality, it's been a challenge for me to master the discipline of this key *2-Minute Leader* practice. But the more I make it a habit, the more I recognize the value. Checking my bearings and making necessary adjustments means different things at different times. Today, the priority may be looking at a trend in the marketplace that my company addresses or at some noteworthy development in the community my church serves. Tomorrow, the priority could shift to internal concerns. For example, I may check the conditions and see that morale is low for some reason or another. I have to ask why and respond wisely. Perhaps I have to distinguish complaints from warnings because a leader must discourage complaints but encourage warnings. Why? Because complaints can damage on-board morale but warnings heeded can keep the corporate ship from sinking. In either case, adjustment is needed.

At the heart of this practice is the place and the priority of change. As I typed that word "change" I recalled both a famous quote and a famous phrase. The quotation is by General Eric Shinseki, U.S. Army Chief of Staff, who said, "If you don't like change, you're going to like irrelevance even less."[1] In contrast, we all know the familiar phrase: "Nobody likes change but a baby." Which of these statements do you most readily associate with? The majority of people will gravitate to the latter. Leaders, however, must embrace change. The wise leader learns to recognize that change does not equate to instability, lack of control, inconvenience or discomfort. I used to make those associations, but no longer. I have grown to see not only the value of change but its necessity in my life and leadership.

Sir Francis Bacon wrote, "If we are to achieve results never before accomplished, we must expect to employ methods never before attempted."[2] My fellow leader, perhaps that can start with the mastery of this two-minute practice of checking your bearings and adjusting as needed. The adjustment may be simple and straightforward—perhaps a brief, course-correcting conversation with a colleague. But it just might be a radical re-direction like the accomplished

> *The wise leader learns to recognize that change does not equate to instability, lack of control, inconvenience or discomfort.*

church builder I met—a man who was willing to push the reset button on his entire career. Whatever change is called for—small or large—the imperative is to stay alert, stay aware and stay ready to do whatever you need to do.

> *"Whatever change is called for—small or large—the imperative is to stay alert, stay aware and stay ready to do whatever you need to do."*

Practice #9
PERSEVERING
Name It and Declaim It.
Identify whatever threatens to pull you down
and deny its power over you.

It is an inescapable fact: As a leader you will face big and troubling things from time to time—things that can shake your confidence or undermine your effectiveness unless you meet them head on. The culprits can be any number of things: conflicts between co-workers, cash flow challenges, downturns in the market, looming deadlines—and those are examples just from my own experience! You could undoubtedly add more to this list from your life as a leader.

When faced with forces that can't be ignored I find that I often get a feeling of desperation. I used to chide myself for responding in that way, but I've learned that desperation can be my best friend. Too often we associate desperation with fear or a sense of being out of control. But I must say that while there is a negative side, I have also discovered that when leveraged properly in my life desperation can be a great aid to me as a leader. In fact, it can be a tool that helps me reach my full potential. I know this may seem counter-intuitive, but consider these benefits, drawn from my own experience:

1. Desperation reminds me of my inadequacies and leads me to rely more on God.

2. Desperation gives birth to creativity, paving a way to places where new solutions can be found.

3. Desperation forces me to slow down and think instead of reacting reflexively.

4. Desperation reminds me of the need for collaborative approaches.

5. Desperation fosters a grateful spirit by reminding me of the good times.

6. Desperation enables me to take advantage of my teammates' skills and expertise.

7. Desperation compels me to work harder and smarter.

8. Desperation drives me to strive for constant improvement and better execution of my assignments.

9. Desperation reveals that my success does not depend exclusively on me.

10. Desperation opens channels for God to work in my life and bring him honor.

So, let me ask: Are you desperate? If so, I hope you recognize that it can be a very good thing indeed. The key is to persevere by enacting—as often as needed—this *2-Minute Leader* practice: **Name It and Declaim It.** Identify whatever threatens to pull you down and deny its power over you.

Perhaps you're struggling to remember what it means to "declaim" something. You're not alone in that, of course. But *declaim* is a word worth remembering. It means to communicate in an impassioned and forceful manner. When you're up against a challenge, don't shrink back from it, don't attempt to go around it, and don't ignore it. See it for what it is and

> *Are you desperate? If so, I hope you recognize that it can be a very good thing indeed.*

declaim against it. I realize that this may seem simplistic; but I can assure you that it has worked time and time again in my various roles as a leader.

I am inspired by leaders who refuse to allow obstacles to permanently block their progress. One of my favorites is long-time NBA head coach Doug Collins. He has led a number of teams, and every time he has taken on a new assignment he has said no to the naysayers and denied the decriers. There's no question that he knows how to turn a team around. In his first season with the Chicago Bulls, the win total increased by 10 games. With the Detroit Pistons the first season increase was 18 games; same in his initial run with the Washington Wizards; and he kept the streak going with the Philadelphia 76ers. Doug Collins simply knows how to identify the threats to success and deny their power. How has he

> *I am inspired by leaders who refuse to allow obstacles to permanently block their progress.*

done it? What can we draw from his experience that is transferable to us as fellow leaders? In reading a feature story on Collins in *Sports Illustrated*[1] I recognized several factors:

1. Masterful Memory. Doug Collins has a photographic recollection of the things that matter to him—nearly every play of every game he has been a part of, countless Bible verses, and, of course, the people he has known in his 60+ years of life. For the most part, this ability has been a blessing; but it is also a challenge because Collins has a hard time forgetting painful things.

2. Innovative Improvisation. Collins has honed a remarkable ability for uncanny, creative play-calling right in the midst of the most intense games. He has at times gotten ahead of himself as a leader, with players who've become frustrated because they have difficulty keeping up with their coach's mind.

3. Exuberant Expression. Known for his generous, deep appreciation for his staff and players, Collins told the *SI* reporter, "I want them to feel important."[2] Ironically this has at times created problems when Collins would "invest" in his players after losses, verbally replaying the game. Many players, not wanting to be reminded, would tune him out.

4. Disciplined Delegation. By the time of his fourth stop in his professional coaching career Collins had learned to trust his assistants and delegate to them almost the entire defensive strategy. He had determined to ensure that his young players not get an "overdose" of his coaching.

Doug Collins has had more than his share of jarring losses and near misses. He was a player on the ill-fated 1972 U.S. Olympic basketball team that was unjustly robbed of the gold medal. He was the first player picked in the 1973 NBA Draft but had to retire at age 29 due to injuries, just two years before his team won the NBA championship. The year after he was let go as coach of the Chicago Bulls, that team won the first of their six NBA titles behind superstar Michael Jordan.

But Collins says that he considers himself a winner in spite of setbacks. When faced with a challenge, he sees it for what it is—an opportunity to persevere, no matter how the circumstances play out. As a leader, I am tremendously encouraged by his example. He wouldn't state it in exactly these words, but Doug Collins has learned how to name it and declaim it.

The power to persevere is crucial. Whenever I have the opportunity to speak to leaders—especially young or emerging leaders—I emphasize this fact. But I tell them that perseverance should always be balanced by the right perspective. Some leaders persevere simply because they are so doggedly determined and will even use other people as their personal stepping stones to get where they want to go. The wise, balanced leader operates with a healthy view of situations, people and leadership itself. How is this expressed? For me, it comes down to 12 key lessons I strive to remember:

1. Leadership is a constant struggle between serving self vs. serving others. Every human being is inclined to act in self-interest; but we exist to serve others, not ourselves. Leadership is, paradoxically, driven by a spirit of servantship.

> *The wise, balanced leader operates with a healthy view of situations, people and leadership itself.*

2. People are led more effectively with inspiration than with information. Leaders who depend on the weight of information often find that it merely weighs others down. Leaders who inspire will lift others up.

3. Leaders must guard against rushing to judgment. Getting the facts straight is essential to getting the decision right.

4. There is great power in simple praise. Leaders who pay attention to the seemingly small things will reap great rewards.

5. Climbing out on a limb is sometimes needful in order to get to the most promising fruit. Leadership can be a risky business. Sometimes, leaders who climb out on a limb will suffer a painful fall; but true leaders are willing to face such possibilities.

6. If you don't *prepare*, chances are you will have to *repair*. Leaders who attempt to take on projects or challenges without adequate contemplation or preparation will inevitably end up fixing something that has gone wrong because of their lack of diligence.

7. Whether it comes naturally or by sheer will power, leaders are readers. Leaders who are not naturally inclined to read must force themselves to do so because the effort is always worth it.

8. Don't waste your time or others' time. Time is your most valuable commodity, and once it's gone, it's gone.

9. Hold on, but hold your tongue. An outburst of temper can destroy a stockpile of influence.

10. What you say "No" to is often more important than what you say "Yes" to. Leaders reveal their true priorities in their *Yes* and *No* decisions.

11. Leadership can be lonely. There are great perks, but there's also a great price; and many are unwilling to pay it.

12. Don't let anyone tell you that you can't do something. God can do extraordinary things through ordinary people who persevere in his strength.

What is facing you right now? Is something—or someone—threatening to derail your leadership? Whatever confronts you must be confronted, but in the right way and with the right attitude.

Practice #10
CELEBRATING
ACT Positively.
Acknowledge excellence.
Celebrate achievement.
Transform relationships.

In the late 1940s, when the U.S. was still regaining its strength in the aftermath of World War II, a tall, boyish preacher with an engaging North Carolina drawl captured the nation's attention. Unlike flamboyant evangelists who seem to stir as much contempt as they do attention, this young man was different. He was simple, direct, and able to connect with people of all ages and all walks of life. His message, the age-old Gospel of Jesus Christ, was delivered with a clarity and power that was almost palpable. It wasn't hypnotic or theatrical; but it was absolutely riveting. When he called upon his listeners to put their trust in Jesus and receive God's gift of salvation, people responded—thousands upon thousands upon thousands of them. In just a few, brief years, he had gone from delivering God's Word in churches to proclaiming it in jam-packed stadiums.

Today, more than six decades since he burst onto the scene, Billy Graham is the world's most revered and respected Christian leader. He has personally communicated the Gospel message to more people in more places than any other person in history. Every U.S. President since Harry S. Truman has sought out the wise counsel of this godly man. At the dedication of the Billy Graham Library in Charlotte, North Carolina, former President George H. W. Bush called him "a gift to the nation and to the world."[1] Few would disagree. As I walked through the halls of the Graham Library on a recent visit I was impressed by the fact that Billy Graham has never been impressed with himself. In fact, he has always gone the extra mile to express how much he relies on others and rejoices in their gifts and accomplishments.

> *As I walked through the halls of the Graham Library...I was impressed by the fact that Billy Graham has never been impressed with himself.*

The core team that Billy Graham built way back in the 1940s stayed with him for his entire, eventful career. Cliff Barrows served as music director of the vast crusade choirs; George Beverly Shea was the featured soloist at all Graham events, radio broadcasts and television specials; Grady Wilson was Graham's first associate evangelist and remained so until his death in 1987; Sherwood Wirt was founding editor of the Graham association's *Decision* magazine. Wirt came on board in the 1950s and stayed at his post until his retirement.

How did Billy Graham assemble and hold together such a formidable team, even as it became increasingly larger over the years? None of these individuals were pushovers or also-rans; they were strong personalities in their own right, both talented and bright. I think the key to Graham's success in keeping his team cohesive lies in the fact that he always acted so positively toward them. As I began crafting this chapter, there was no question that Billy Graham was to me the ideal example of this *2-Minute Leader* practice: ***ACT Positively: Acknowledge excel-***

lence. Celebrate achievement. Transform relationships. Consistently and with genuine regard, Graham took note when a team member was especially effective on a major project. He was quick to acknowledge work done well. But he didn't stop there. He gave honor when honor was due, both publicly and privately. As a result, he transformed relationships into life-long partnerships. Graham is known universally as a compelling evangelist; he is practically unknown as a phenomenal recruiter, builder and leader of teams that have stood the test of time.

Let's unpack some of the treasures hidden in this *2-Minute Leader* practice:

Acknowledge excellence. When someone on your team is doing a superb job, do you notice? Do you then take the next step and tell them? Perhaps you've heard the story of the taciturn farmer whose wife threatened to leave him unless he agreed to go through marriage counseling. He relented; and at the start of the first session the counselor asked, "Do you love your wife?" The farmer replied, "Of course I love my wife. I told her that when we got married, and if

I ever change my mind I'll be sure to let her know." Regrettably, a lot of leaders are like that mule-headed farmer: they tell a team member at the outset that they're doing a good job, and if that ever changes they will let the person know differently. This may sound extreme, but I assure you it is all too common.

Excellence must be observed to be acknowledged, so the first priority is to truly pay attention. Don't get so absorbed in your job and your projects that you lose sight of the people around you—particularly the people who look to you for leadership. It is only normal for those who expect you to lead to also expect you to encourage. Ever notice what toddlers say more often than anything else? "Look at me! Look at me!" The harsh truth is that embedded in human nature is the desire to be seen and appreciated by other people. This is not an inherent weakness; it is

> *Excellence must be observed to be acknowledged, so the first priority is to truly pay attention.*

simply the way we are wired. So, my fellow leader, pay attention and be constantly on the look-out for exceptional performance. And, when you see it, point it out and say "great job...thanks...awesome..." or whatever is appropriate to the occasion.

When you learn to look at others in the right way—with positive expectations and eager desire for their success—the impact can be deep. It can even extend well beyond your own team and your own sphere of influence. Billy Graham, a son of the South, grew up in the midst of a culture steeped in racism. From childhood he witnessed the extreme divide between whites and blacks. When the civil rights movement began to gather momentum in the mid-1950s, Graham dared to encourage integrated seating at all of his events. He took special notice of the brilliance and excellence of one man in particular—a fellow minister of the Gospel, Rev. Martin Luther King, Jr. At Graham's 1957 breakthrough evangelistic campaign in New York City, he invited Rev. King to join him on the platform at Madison Square Garden. It was the beginning of an unusual friendship.

Several years later, Billy Graham posted bail for Rev. King after the civil rights leader was jailed during a non-violent protest in Birmingham, Alabama. Graham's own life demonstrates that honestly and faithfully observing other people—especially colleagues and peers—can change one's thinking and radically alter one's attitudes.

Acknowledging excellence is always a positive thing to do, but it must be coupled with the second part of this crucial *2-Minute Leader* practice: Celebrate achievement.

Celebrate achievement. A man I greatly admire, Dr. John C. Maxwell, has been called "the dean of Christian leadership." Rightly so. He has pastored

> *Billy Graham took special notice of the brilliance and excellence of one man in particular—a fellow minister of the Gospel, Rev. Martin Luther King, Jr.*

mega-churches, formed mega-organizations and authored mega-bestsellers—most of them on the subject of leadership. I was privileged to work for Dr. Maxwell for many years and I can tell you from first-hand experience, he is masterful in celebrating achievement. If you're on his team, and you're doing an exceptional job, you will be appreciated and your achievements will be celebrated. This ought not to be unusual; it ought to be the norm. And it will be the norm for leaders who operate from a positive perspective. I have seen the other extreme as a team member. I once had a boss who had a standard reply to anyone who ever told him that he looked tired. With a stern face he would say, "I didn't know there was another option." Whenever I heard that I would instantly think, *Well, of course, there are other options!* He was a brilliant man, but those moments of negativity kept him down and brought others down.

As a leader it is important that I strive constantly to be at my best. When I'm not, I know it and so does my team. If I'm drained of energy, others will be affected. If, for whatever reason, I'm lapsing into a negative state, it's time for a readjustment because I know it will prevent me from seeing others as I should and celebrating their achievements as I must. I've learned to recognize the warning signs of encroaching negativity...

1. I can't remember the last time I felt an intimacy with God. I have become too busy or too distracted for a daily time of silence and being alone with him—not just for me to make requests of him, but also for him to speak into my life.

2. I have a low level of energy, a physical tiredness that just seems to hang on.

3. My patience with people is thin, preventing me from showing grace toward others or providing solutions for them. If anything, I'm adding to the problems.

> *"...A negative state...will prevent me from seeing others as I should and celebrating their achievements as I must."*

4. I over-react to minor offenses. I give a "3" offense a "9" response.

5. Building relationships with my team members has been marginalized and put on the back burner.

6. My family is being neglected. Other people are getting my best, not those to whom I should be closest.

7. I'm not making time for physical exercise.

8. I'm letting things fall through the cracks.

9. I've become a poor listener to people who deserve my full attention.

10. I'm insensitive to the plight of poor or hurting people. My tank of compassion is running on fumes.

Well, those are my warning signs. Can you relate? When I see these indicators popping up in my life and leadership, I know that I have to immediately begin making changes. I encourage you to make your own list of warning signs, or simply adopt this one. And then promise yourself (as I continue to promise myself) that when you sense a lapse in your life or your leadership you will take it to heart and put it to practice. You cannot lead positively unless you are living positively.

> *You cannot lead positively unless you are living positively.*

Now, the third element of our *2-Minute Leader* practice: Transform relationships.

Transform relationships. This one is completely different from the first two points because it is not something to do but something to be experienced. It is the result of the first two parts of this practice. When you as a leader acknowledge the excellence and celebrate the achievement of others, you will see a transformational effect on yourself, your colleagues and your entire team.

We noted earlier that Billy Graham is by nature a person who appreciates and values others, but he also made a conscious decision to focus on what he does best and build a team of others he then liberated to do their best. As they have done so, he has acknowledged their excellence, celebrated their achievements

> *When you as a leader acknowledge the excellence and celebrate the achievement of others, you will see a transformational effect on yourself, your colleagues and your entire team.*

and seen the relationships with them transformed into something extraordinary. The Graham Team, all pulling together under their esteemed leader, have reached a cumulative audience of 2.2 billion people. The success may have begun with Billy Graham, but it has had an impact on the entire world.

Don't ever underestimate the power of positive action in your leadership. Pay attention, show appreciation, express admiration and celebrate the achievements of others. The results, I promise, will truly be transformational.

CONCLUSION

Over the years, I have written hundreds of blog posts. Some that I had expected to capture attention ended up falling flat. Other posts for which I had limited expectations soared to unimaginable heights. I have tried to figure out what is certain to resonate with readers, but I've concluded that there is simply no way to predict the response. There was, however, one blog post that I had written with high hopes …and it got exactly the reception that I desired. In fact, it was passed along thousands of times via email, tweets and Facebook postings. That post—titled "I Have Found the Perfect Leader"—captures so many important thoughts about leadership that I had originally intended to use it in the introduction to this book. I made that attempt but realized that it would be more apropos to the conclusion. Here is that original post...

I Have Found The Perfect Leader

I came across a blog post today extolling the virtues of the "perfect dessert." I'm a sucker for a great dessert but it doesn't really add value to my life (in fact, it adds something I don't need any more of). But that word "perfect" got me to thinking about perfection in other categories. Inevitably, that led to my favorite topic—leadership—and the possibility of finding the perfect leader. What would be the characteristics and the character of that person? Does such a person exist? The answer is a resounding *Yes*. Here's what I discovered about the Perfect Leader...

1. The perfect leader sees not just what I am but what I can become.

2. The perfect leader builds an inner circle to equip and inspire.

3. The perfect leader exercises formidable people skills.

4. The perfect leader operates with both short-term and long-term strategies.

5. The perfect leader is under authority but also exercises authority.

6. The perfect leader has a succession plan.

7. The perfect leader is my best friend.

8. The perfect leader covers for my mistakes and doesn't hold them against me.

9. The perfect leader has unlimited resources to pour into my life.

10. The perfect leader is extravagantly generous.

11. The perfect leader is a joy to be with.

12. The perfect leader comforts me in tough and trying times.

13. The perfect leader equips me with a great training manual.

14. The perfect leader looks at what people are on the inside, not just what they are on the outside.

15. The perfect leader can build bridges with anyone.

16. The perfect leader protects his people from utter failure.

17. The perfect leader guides to a clear career path.

18. The perfect leader constantly challenges.

19. The perfect leader invariably surprises in wonderful ways.

20. The perfect leader brings joy and makes his followers laugh.

21. The perfect leader encourages his friends to look to the future.

22. The perfect leader argues on behalf of those to whom he is closest.

23. The perfect leader is creative in the truest sense of the word.

24. The perfect leader would die for his team.

25. The perfect leader has so many more qualities that an unlimited number of chapters couldn't adequately describe him.

I met this Perfect Leader in 1980 and I've been following him ever since. His name is Jesus Christ.

———————

My hope and prayer is that you have sensed the influence of this Perfect Leader throughout the pages of this book. I have no higher purpose than to follow him, serve him and do his will all the days of my life. If you know him intellectually or historically but not in a personal, vibrant way, I encourage you to trust in him. I leave you with the words he used to describe himself: "I am the way and the truth and the life. No one comes to the Father except through me."[1]

DEDICATION

TO SONYA

Extraordinary wife.

Remarkable mother.

Servant leader.

Sacrificial example.

Formidable organizer.

Trusted friend.

Time master.

Resourceful steward.

Tireless worker.

Need meeter.

Hope giver.

Wise King Solomon said,
*"He who finds a wife finds what is good
and receives favor from the Lord."*
I couldn't agree more.

REFERENCES

CHAPTER 1
[1] *Fast Company*, June 2011

CHAPTER 2
[1] *Business Week*, May 25, 1998
[2] Mark 11:23

CHAPTER 3
[1] Matthew 9:9a
[2] Matthew 9:9b
[3] Matthew 9:9c
[4] Matthew 9:10
[5] Matthew 9:11
[6] Matthew 9:12
[7] Matthew 9:13

CHAPTER 5
[1] *USA Today*, November 12, 2010
[2] *USA Today*, August 26, 2011
[3] Ibid.
[4] Ibid.

CHAPTER 7
[1] 1 Chronicles 28:2b
[2] Acts 13:36
[3] 1 Chronicles 28:2b
[4] 1 Chronicles 28:2c

[5] 1 Chronicles 28:19
[6] 1 Chronicles 29:2-5a
[7] 1 Chronicles 29:5b
[8] 1 Chronicles 29:6-8a
[9] 1 Chronicles 29:9
[10] *Sports Illustrated*, March 7, 2011
[11] Ibid.
[12] Ibid.

CHAPTER 8
[1] *The New York Times*, November 10, 2009
[2] GoodReads.com

CHAPTER 9
[1] *Sports Illustrated*, April 11, 2011
[2] Ibid.

CHAPTER 10
[1] Speech given by former President George H. W. Bush at dedication ceremonies of the Billy Graham Library, Charlotte, NC, May 31, 2007

CONCLUSION
[1] John 14:6